Rangers

Mike Wilson

Published in association with The Basic Skills Agency

Hodder & Stoughton

A MEMBER OF THE HODDER HEADLINE GROUP

Acknowledgements

Photos: pp. 5, 10, 26, 34, 36, 40 © Action Images, p. 19 © Coloursport, p. 44 reproduced with kind permission of Rangers FC.

Cover photo: © Allsport.

Orders: please contact Bookpoint Ltd, 39 Milton Park, Abingdon, Oxon OX14 4TD. Telephone: (44) 01235 400414, Fax: (44) 01235 400454. Lines are open from 9.00–6.00, Monday to Saturday, with a 24 hour message answering service. Email address: orders@bookpoint.co.uk

British Library Cataloguing in Publication Data
A catalogue record for this title is available from The British Library

ISBN 0 340 71168 X

First published 1998
Impression number 10 9 8 7 6 5 4 3 2
Year 2003 2002 2001 2000 1999

Typeset by Fakenham Photosetting Ltd, Fakenham, Norfolk.
Printed in Great Britain for Hodder & Stoughton Educational, a division of Hodder Headline Plc, 338 Euston Road, London NW1 3BH by Redwood Books, Trowbridge, Wiltshire.

Contents

This is the story of Rangers Football Club.

It was early in 1872
when a team of young men
met on Glasgow Green.
They came to play football.

One of the men,
Moses McNeil,
named the new team Rangers.
It was the name
of an English Rugby team
he had heard about.

If you grow up in Glasgow,
football is religion.
And religion is football.

If you are a Catholic,
your team is Celtic.
If you are a Protestant,
your team is Rangers.

Together,
they are the Old Firm.

Always big rivals,
sometimes bitter enemies.

In Glasgow,
Rangers and Celtic
have ruled in football
for over 100 years.

1 Early Days

1872 was early days for Scottish football.

There were only a few proper teams
in Scotland.
There was no Scottish FA yet.
The Scottish Cup was only in its first year.

Rangers FC did not have a ground yet.
And at first, they wore hooped jerseys,
(just like Celtic!),
not the famous light blue shirts.

But in their first few matches,
Rangers really made people sit up
and take notice.
They held their own,
against the top teams of the day.

Their first ever match was in 1873.
It was against a top team
called Vale of Leven.
Vale of Leven should have made mince-meat
of the new young team.
But the match was a draw.

And even when Rangers lost a match,
the fans cheered them on.
They always played
with such fire and passion.

Rangers did not move to Ibrox until 1887.
Their first ground was at Burnbank.
Rangers stayed there for just one year.
Then they moved to Kinning Park in 1876.

That season,
they were in the Scottish Cup Final
for the first time.
The club was just five years old.

They were playing Vale of Leven again.
That was the team they had met
in their very first game.

Like that match,
the Cup Final was a draw.

Ibrox stadium.

The two teams played a replay.
That was a draw as well.
But it should have been 2–1 to Rangers.
The ref didn't spot a goal
scored by Rangers in extra time!

A rocket shot by a Rangers player
called Willie Dunlop
flew into the Leven's net.
But then it hit the legs
of a man in the crowd
and bounced out again,
to the Leven's goal-keeper.

The goalie booted the ball
back up the field.
The ref shouted play on!
And the match was a draw!

Two years later, in 1879,
Rangers met Vale of Leven
in the Scottish Cup Final
yet again.
Yet again, it was a 1–1 draw!
And yet again,
Rangers had a winning goal disallowed.
This time for off-side.

The Rangers players were furious.
They refused to play in the replay,
set for one week later.

So Vale of Leven kicked off and
walked the ball up the empty pitch
to the empty Rangers goal,
and rolled it over the line.

It was the softest goal
the Rangers defence has ever let in!

So Rangers still hadn't won a Cup Final.
No matter.

Two weeks after that defeat,
they met Vale of Leven
(yet again!)
in the Glasgow Charity Cup.

This time, Rangers won 2–1.
This was the first of many trophies
that Rangers would carry home.

In 1890–91,
the Scottish Football League began.
At the end of the very first season,
Rangers finished joint-top
with Dumbarton.

The two teams drew the play-off match,
so both teams got joint-winners' medals.

By the 1890s, Rangers' big rival
was not Vale of Leven any more.

It was Celtic.

Rangers beat them 3–1
in the Glasgow Cup in 1893.
Then they beat them 3–1 again
in the Scottish Cup Final of 1894.

2 The Best Rangers Team of All?

Many Rangers teams could claim
to be the best Rangers team of them all.

But the Rangers team that won the League
in 1898–99
have a special claim to fame.

They won all of their League matches that season.
They didn't drop a single point,
and they got to three Cup Finals
that season too.
(But they lost them all . . .)

No other football club in the world
can claim a league record like that.
So maybe they were the best Rangers team
there has ever been!

Rangers v Celtic: the 'Old Firm'.

In 1909, Rangers and Celtic
met in the Scottish Cup Final.

Once again,
it was a match that nobody won.
This time,
it was the famous Hampden Park Riots.

The Final was a draw.
So was the replay.

At the end of the replay,
some of the players
wanted to leave the field.
But some wanted to stay on
and play extra time.
That's what the fans wanted too.
They spilled onto the pitch.

Pretty soon,
they began smashing up the ground.
They set fire to the buildings,
and threw sticks and stones at the police.

The match was abandoned,
and there were no winners that year.
For once, Rangers and Celtic were united.
They were united in sadness,
shock and shame.

The 1920s and 1930s were a good time
to be a Rangers fan.

The club won the League
15 times between 1920 and 1939.
And if they didn't win,
like in 1932, and 1936,
they usually came second.
Just behind Celtic.

In 1920–21,
Rangers ended the season
ten points clear of Celtic,
who were second.
Rangers had won all but one
of their 42 League matches.

Many people said
they were the best Rangers team
of all time!

By 1928,
Rangers had won
the Glasgow Cup 15 times,
and the Charity Cup 11 times.
But the Scottish Cup
always seemed out of reach.

They had had just the three wins:
way back in 1894, 1897 and 1898.

But that year, 1929,
Rangers won the double.
And they did it in fine style!

Celtic were hammered 3–1
in the Scottish Cup Final
and Kilmarnock went down 5–1
as Rangers clinched the League title.

The Rangers team of 1929–30
was called the 'Clean-sweep' team.

This was because they won everything –
every trophy they went in for!
They won the League, of course,
and the Scottish Cup.
They won the Glasgow Cup
and the Charity Cup.
They even won the Second Eleven Cup,
and other minor trophies.

In 1933–34,
Rangers beat the English Champions, Arsenal,
2–0 at Ibrox.
Rangers were named
Champions of Britain.

Many fans said that
this was the best Rangers team
there had ever been!

In fact, Rangers' success rate
slowed down after 1939.
But this was all down to
the start of World War Two (1939–45).

1946–47 was the first season
after the War.
Rangers went back to their winning ways.
It was as if they had never been away.

They won the League.
And they were the first ever winners
of the new League Cup,
when they slammed four goals
past Kilmarnock.

At this time,
the star players were
Willie Waddell and Willie Thornton.
They both started playing for Rangers
at the tender age of 16.

Willie Thornton scored 250 goals for Rangers.
He was a good all-round forward.
But he was famous for being good in the air.
Willie Waddell played on the right wing.
Many times he crossed the ball,
for Willie Thornton to head home.
But Willie Waddell scored 140 goals,
as well as making them for team-mates.

3 Managers

William Wilton
was the first real manager
of Rangers FC.

He became match secretary in 1889.
But really he ran the whole show,
and carried the club to greatness.

That is, until 1920.
That year he drowned
in a tragic accident.

His team coach, Bill Struth, took over,
and the team went from strength to strength.

Bill Struth was manager for 34 years.
When he retired, aged 74, in 1954,
he had led Rangers
to 80 championships, titles and trophies.

Rangers' next manager, Scot Symon,
took the team into Europe.
In fact, they lost their first two
European finals
(both in the European Cup Winners' Cup).

One was against Fiorentina in 1961.
One was against Bayern Munich in 1967.

But by the 1960s,
the message was clear:
Rangers were playing on a world stage.

And their turn would come.

It was in May 1972.
Rangers met Moscow Dynamo
in the European Cup Winners' Cup.

The two sides had met before,
just after World War Two.
At one point in that match,
Rangers were playing against 12 men!
The Russians had put on a substitute,
but nobody came off!
Even against 12 men,
Rangers had still held the Russians
to a 2–2 draw.

Now 26 years later,
the teams met again.
(By now, the Rangers manager
was the famous winger Willie Waddell).

This time, Rangers would not settle for a draw!

Rangers with the European Cup Winners' Cup, 1972.

At half time, Rangers were 2–0 up.
Then, after the break,
Willie Johnstone scored a third.
The Light Blues looked unstoppable.

But then, slowly and surely,
Moscow Dynamo began to get back
into the match.
With three minutes to go,
the score was 3–2 to Rangers.
The stage was set for a nail-biting finish!

But at the final whistle,
Rangers had hung on to their lead.
Rangers' first ever European trophy
came home in triumph to Ibrox.

But the excitement was too much
for some Scottish fans.
They ran on to the pitch,
only to end up in fights
with the local police.

Rangers were banned
from European football for two years.

4 Disaster

Winning the European Cup Winners' Cup
was the best moment
in the history of Rangers Football Club.

For many fans,
it helped them to forget
the worst moment in Rangers' history.

That had happened one year before,
in 1971.

It was 2 January 1971.

A huge crowd of 80,000
were at Ibrox
for the Old Firm game
between Rangers and Celtic.

There had often been crowd trouble
at Old Firm matches.
But this time there was no fighting.
The crowds had been really friendly.
Maybe it was because
the match was heading for a 0–0 draw.

Then, with two minutes to go,
Celtic took the lead.
Rangers fans were stunned.
But the groans turned to cheers
30 seconds later,
when Colin Stein made it 1–1.

Two goals in the last two minutes!
It was unbelievable!
The crowds went mad,
and pushed forward in triumph.

But the steel fences gave way.
Thousands of fans fell forward.
They were crushed together
in the mad rush down the terraces.
Some fell to the ground,
and were walked on by the rest.
The ones at the front were crushed
by the weight of the thousands of people
pressing down from behind.

66 people died.

Once again,
an Old Firm match had ended in disaster.
There were no winners that day,
but thousands of losers.

In the mid-1980s,
Rangers slipped a little.

For four seasons (1982–86),
they could only finish 4th or 5th
in the League.

Players came and went.
(Ally McCoist came from Sunderland.
He cost only £185,000,
but he would be worth his weight in gold!)

Managers came and went.
(Jock Wallace was Rangers' manager twice,
and he resigned twice –
in 1978 and 1986.)

And people came and went
on the Board of Governors.
(David Holmes took over as Chairman
and began to bring the club up to date.)

True – from 1981–1989,
Rangers were in every League Cup Final,
and won six of them . . .
But – Rangers had no luck in Europe . . .
No Scottish Cup wins since 1981 . . .
And they were finishing
4th or 5th in the League every year.

It just wasn't good enough!

5 Graeme Souness

Rangers were in danger
of becoming just another ordinary side.

They were saved by one man –
Graeme Souness.

His over-night success at Rangers
was just as amazing
as the success of his old team-mate
Kevin Keegan,
when he went to Newcastle.
But Souness did it first!

Graeme Souness
became player-manager of Rangers
early in April 1986.

Chairman David Holmes said:
'I started thinking –
who did I want to work with
to make Rangers a world-class team?
Graeme Souness was the first name on the list.'

Graeme Souness.

When Walter Smith joined Souness
on the bench,
David knew he had a winning team!

At the end of the 1985–86 season,
Rangers finished 5th in the League.
Their worst ever League position
was 6th – and that was in 1926.

At the start of the next season,
the new player-manager
told the fans not to expect too much.
But the fans had high hopes
as Graeme Souness took the field
for the first match of the season
against Hibs.

But after 40 minutes,
Souness was sent off!
Rangers struggled on with ten men.

In the last game of that season,
Souness was sent off again!
This time it was against Aberdeen,
but it didn't stop Rangers
from winning the League
in Souness' first full season!

Apart from Graeme Souness,
the team included Ally McCoist,
the goal-scoring machine,
and the England team favourites
Chris Woods and Terry Butcher.

This team could win the League
even when their player-manager was sent off!
They could win the League
with only ten men on the field!

Maybe *this* was the best Rangers team ever!

Graeme Souness always did
what was best for football,
and best for Rangers Football Club.

Rangers players were usually
Scottish, and Protestant.
Sometimes, when he signed players,
Souness broke with tradition.
Rangers fans didn't always like it.

He signed many players from England,
top players like Trevor Francis,
Ray Wilkins and Gary Stevens.

He signed Mark Walters,
the first black player
ever to play in Scotland.

But the fans could not complain
when all these great new players
helped Rangers to a 5–1 win over Celtic
in August 1988!

But the biggest upset came
when Graeme Souness signed Mo Johnston.

Season tickets were ripped up.
Flags and scarves were burned
on the Ibrox terraces.
Fans said they would stop supporting Rangers
unless Souness resigned.

And the reason why Mo Johnston
was so unpopular?
He was a Catholic.
Even worse, he had been a Celtic player.

For many die-hard Rangers fans,
this was the worst crime.

But for Souness,
football – and football skills –
were far more important than religion,
and old hatred.

And when Johnston
scored two cracking goals
for Rangers against his old club,
even the die hard Rangers fans
began to forgive him!

Graeme Souness
had changed Rangers for good.
His changes meant
that the world famous 'Nine In A Row'
was possible.
Celtic had won the League
nine times in a row (1966–74).
Rangers wanted to do the same.
But the pressure was too much.

Souness argued with linesmen
at Rangers matches.
He was banned from the touchlines
for a year.
So was his assistant, Walter Smith.

Then Souness split up from his wife
and his children.

Then he had to have a heart operation.
The stress of the top job
in Scottish football
was getting too much for him.

In April 1991,
Graeme Souness left Rangers.
He went to Liverpool,
and steered them to a Cup Final win
in 1992.

When Graeme Souness left for Liverpool,
he asked Walter Smith to go with him.
'We make a winning team,' he said.

Smith told him: 'no'.
He'd stick it out with Rangers.
It was probably the best decision
Walter Smith would ever make!

He carried on
where Graeme Souness had left off –
leading Rangers to one League Championship
after another.

Walter Smith made a new winning team –
with new Rangers Chairman,
David Murray.

Murray took over in 1988,
and began spending millions on the club.
He has spent £30 million
on the ground alone,
to make Ibrox quite simply
one of the best grounds in Europe.

But it's the players that have made Rangers
what they are today.
They've been scoring goals
and winning matches,
week after week, year after year!

6 Ally McCoist

Manager Walter Smith
has called him 'lucky'.
But there's nothing lucky
about Ally McCoist.
It's all down to hard work,
raw talent and a hunger for goals.

He is Rangers' top goal scorer
in the past ten years
with a grand total of over 140 goals.
No-one else comes near that total.

For about a year,
under Graeme Souness,
Ally was on the subs' bench.
So when new manager Walter Smith
gave him a second chance,
Ally really made up for lost time!

He scored nine goals in six games.

Ally McCoist.

Mark Hateley has been
Ally's best striking partner.
Once, in two seasons together,
they scored 140 goals!

In 1992–93,
Ally scored 49 goals,
one short of his 50.
But a broken leg ended his hopes
of a dream season.

Still, he's got an MBE to his name now.

And there are only three Rangers players
who have been with the club
for all of the Nine In A Row
League Championships.
Ally McCoist is one of them.

And he is more proud of that
than anything.

Brian Laudrup.

7 Brian Laudrup

Brian Laudrup is from Denmark.
He came to Rangers
from Italian club Fiorentina,
in 1994.

He was ready for a change
after the high pressure
of top Italian football.

In Italy, the fans turn nasty
if you have one bad game.
But at Rangers,
the fans gave Brian time to settle in.
They told him: keep plugging away.
We know you'll be a great player
and do great things for Rangers.

That was when Brian knew
he had joined a special club
with special fans.

And the fans were right.
By the end of his first season,
Brian was Player of the Year in Scotland!

Brian has said:
'I have always enjoyed making goals,
just as much as scoring them.'
And with Mark Hateley
and Ally McCoist up front,
Brian has helped to make
hundreds of goals for Rangers!

But he did score one important goal himself:
On 7 May 1997,
Brian Laudrup scored the only goal
in a match against Dundee.

That goal won the match,
the League Championship,
and the famous Nine In A Row.

8 Paul Gascoigne

Gazza joined Rangers in July 1995.
He was going nowhere in Italy.
He had been hit by injury,
and had not really been at his best
for years.

He was hoping to return to his best football.
And that's what the Rangers fans wanted too!

In the last game but one
of his first season in Scottish football,
Gazza scored a hat-trick
in a 3–1 win over Aberdeen.
Rangers had won
their 8th League Championship in a row.

Gazza had scored 19 goals that season,
and he was Player of the Year.
Once he'd scored his first goal for Rangers
– against Celtic of course –
there was no stopping him!

Paul Gascoigne.

9 Dick Advocaat

In September 1998,
manager Walter Smith left Ibrox.
Dick Advocaat took over.

He spent over £20 million
on new players.
Players like Colin Hendrie, the Scottish captain,
who was brought home to Scotland.

Celtic might have won the league in 97–98.
But Rangers led the way
right from the start of the 98–99 season.

They were only a handful of points clear
– not like the ten or twenty points lead
they'd had in some seasons.

But it was enough.
Rangers were back on top.
Back where they belonged!

10 The Best Rangers Team of Them All?

The Rangers team of 1992–93
won 44 games on the trot.
They went for seven months
without a defeat.

This was the team
that won the League Championship
for the 5th time in a row.
They finished nine points clear
at the top of the table,
and they lost only four of their 44 matches
in the League that season.

Many fans said
this was the best Rangers team of all time!
And this was before Gazza,
before Brian Laudrup,
before Jorg Albertz.

In 1994–95,
the season that Laudrup came to Glasgow,
Rangers finished 15 points clear.

In 1996–97,
with Paul Gascoigne on board,
Rangers won the Championship
by five points, with a match to spare.

Celtic had won Nine In A Row
in 1966–74.
Now, at last,
that record had been matched.
Rangers won Nine In A Row
in classic style in 1996–97.
And best of all,
they beat Celtic four times that season!

That Rangers team must be
one of the best there has ever been.
But there have been so many
great Rangers sides,
over the years . . .

Which do *you* think
is the best Rangers team of them all?

The 1997–98 Rangers squad.